FOCUS

PHOENIX MARCÓN, CHC, CLC

FOCUS

How to Optimize your Vision through Strategic Steps of Self-Discipline

COPYRIGHT © 2020 BY MARCÓN PRESS

All rights reserved. No part of this publication may be reproduced, distributed, or transmitted in any form or by any means, including photocopying, recording, or other electronic or mechanical methods, without the prior written permission of the publisher, except in the case of brief quotations embodied in critical reviews and certain other noncommercial uses permitted by copyright law. For permission requests, write to the publisher, addressed "Attention: Permissions Coordinator," at the address below.

Printed by Marcón Press
Cover Design by Marcón Press
Layout Design by Marcón Press
Prepared for Printing by Marcón Press
Author Contact: PO. Box 737 | Allen, TX 75002
PHOENON.com

Library Congress Cataloging-in-Publication Data
Marcón, Phoenix
FOCUS/Phoenix Marcón. p. cm.
1. Self-Help 2. Mind and Body 3. Reference

Paperback - ISBN 978-1-952681-24-0

eBook - ISBN 978-1-952681-23-3

10 9 8 7 6 5 4 3 2 1

First Edition

DISCLAIMER NOTICE

Please note the information contained within this document is for educational and entertainment purposes only. Every attempt has been made to provide accurate, up to date and reliable complete information. No warranties of any kind are expressed or implied. Readers acknowledge that the author is not engaging in the rendering of legal, financial, medical, or professional advice.

By reading this document, the reader agrees that under no circumstances are we responsible for any losses, direct or indirect, which are incurred as a result of the use of information contained within this document, including, but not limited to, errors, omissions, or inaccuracies.

OTHER BOOKS BY PHOENIX MARCÓN

FICTION:	CARNATION
SELF-HELP:	LUMINARIES, vol. I-II
	LUMINARIES - Pocket of Inspiration
	Empower
	Money
	Stress
	Productivity
	Focus
	Mindset
	Focus
	Confidence
	Purpose
	Affirmation
	Meaning
HEALTH:	START HERE - Ketogenics for Beginners
	The FOOLPROOF Keto Diet
POETRY:	Thoughts of Wonder
BUSINESS:	Better Business Book (co-authored)
	Entrepreneurial Hustle
	Modern Hustle
	Cryptocurrency Defined
	Blockchain Defined
	CIO Defined
	FBA Fortunes

(Coming Soon)

CULINARY:	Date Night
FICTION:	Beautiful People (Saga)
NON-FICTION:	LUMINARIES, vol. III
	HUMOR: Jocose

More to come...

TABLE OF CONTENTS

Chapter 1
"FOCUS" Defined   13
    Why do people suffer from a lack of focus?   14
    How can you counter a lack of focus?   16
    Types of focus   18
    Inner focus   18
    Focusing on others   18
    Outer focus   19

Chapter 2
Escaping the Busy Trap   21
    Unraveling burnout   23
    Focus to undo the effects of the burnout   23
    The impact of being overwhelmed   24

Chapter 3
Reclaiming Your Time   29
    Poor diet and nutrition   30
    Hormones at play   33
    Lack of sleep   34
    Stress   34
    Lack of physical activity   35
    Surrounding environment   35
    Quality of information   36

Chapter 4
Benefits of Being Focused   39
    Helps take control   40

Yields positive energy	40
Enhances problem-solving skills	41
Instills decision-making skills	42
Removes distractions	42
Gets things done	43
Generates satisfaction	43
Builds momentum	44
Increases engagement	45

Chapter 5
How Highly Successful People Develop Self-Discipline   **47**

Vision	48
Prioritize	48
Say no to distractions	49
Handle one task at a time	49
Divide up goals	50
Rewards and breaks	50
Learn from mistakes	51
Rise above feelings	51
Love what you do	52
Manipulate energy	52

Chapter 6
Strategies to Building Unbreakable Focus   **55**

Train your brain	56
Plan it all out	57
Rest for a while	57
Work with music	58
Practice mindfulness	58
Limit phone usage	59
Give constant reminders	60
Plan your day	60

Brain Updates	61
Enthusiasm	62
Water	62
Cleanliness	62
Theme	63
Rhythm	63

Chapter 7
Why Should You Focus on One Thing at A Time — 65

It gets things done	66
It leaves less room for error	66
Higher success rate	67
It does not deplete energy	68
It keeps distractions away	69
It lets you enjoy work	69

Chapter 8
Online Tools for Laser Focus — 73

Bonus 1
Focus Checklists to Get You Started — 81

Focus for Students	82
Focus for Busy Moms	82
Focus for Working at Home	83
Focus for Creative People	84
Focus at Work	85

Bonus 2
21 Day Focus Challenge — 87

Bonus 3
75+ Ways to Take Action, Stay Focused and Get Motivated — 107

TIPS FOR TAKING ACTION	108
TIPS TO GET MOTIVATED!	131

Chapter 1

"FOCUS" Defined

Focus is integral to accomplishment. It may fall in the same category as ambition, motivation, leadership, and other driving forces behind becoming successful but does not necessarily get the attention that it deserves. Often downplayed, the role of focus cannot be sabotaged in an individual's ability to be productive.

What all this means is that you need to be focused to achieve something or become successful in your endeavors. But before we go into that, here is a look at what focus means.

By definition, focus is a skill that allows people to start a task without procrastination and then keep up their attention and effort until the job is complete. It is an ability to not only pay attention to things that they are engaged in but also avoid distractions that will impede the work they are trying to do.

Focus is so important to getting anything done that you can't think without focus. When you hear about things like perception, memory, learning, reasoning, decision making, and problem-solving, you know that none of these can be done successfully unless you focus.

On the contrary, a wandering mind will make you less effective in your work and your productivity will suffer. The same will also compromise the quality of work giving you less than optimal results. Not to forget that you will also be wasting time every instance your mind drifts off.

Why do people suffer from a lack of focus?

In some cases, a lack of focus may be a matter of interest. Take your everyday to-do list for instance. Not everything on the list might be interesting to work on, but needs to get done anyways for you to move ahead. In these instances, you may find yourself stuck, trapped doing something that you couldn't care less about. Your only obligation may be the feeling that you need to get the job done to move on to other things. Not such a great motivator, but that's reality; in the real-world, things need to get done to make way for other things.

It is only natural that your mind starts to drift off in these situations. You may end up finding excuses for not doing that particular thing, say by justifying that you don't *need* to do the job right then, or that it's not *that* important or even something like you've got *better things* to do than the job on hand. But any way you dress them up, they are all just excuses for procrastination.

Which brings us to another aspect of focus, procrastination. Procrastination is perhaps the biggest hurdle in the way of attaining good focus. When you use procrastination to get out of things what you are saying is that you don't want to do a particular task, or that you are secretly hoping that it will just go away on its own, or that you will *eventually* feel motivated to do it.

With so much going on, it is no wonder that focus gets sidelined and never surfaces to the forefront.

While a lot more can be said on procrastination, we will cross that bridge when we come to it (in a later chapter). For now, it is sufficient to say that procrastination is the granddaddy of all excuses and will never let you focus properly on any given task.

How can you counter a lack of focus?

Moving on, while you may be well aware of what is stopping you from focusing (think procrastination), you may not know how to tackle this problem. So, here's some help:

- **Address WHAT needs to be done**

    To make focus work for you, you need to have a **clear-cut goal**; call it a grounded purpose towards which all your efforts are directed. When you have this reference point in sight, you can apply all your skillset and decision making to get the job done right. But with this crucial factor missing, you may as well go on a roller coaster ride.

    It is these clear-cut goals that define <u>what</u> needs to get done.

    Clear cut goals also stop you from derailing and prevent you from going places where you never intended to go. Pick out a typical day in your life and think of all the fifty or so things you need to do. With your mind divided and scattered trying to deal with all fifty at the same time, you are likely not going to get much done. On the flip side, you may neglect to do some of the more important ones as you keep thinking about everything else instead.

    This is a point where having the ability to focus effectively can come save your day. Using focus, work using the process of elimination, and prioritize your goals. When you learn to prioritize your goals, you end up spending your time in a more meaningful way; the important stuff gets done first and the not-so-important later on.

Filtering out such time-eaters also helps you regain control over the chaos and you no longer feel that you are wasting time.

- **Address WHY something needs to be done**

    When clear cut goals are paired with a **sense of purpose** the dilemma starts to resolve itself fairly easily. This sense of purpose also verifies why something needs to be done.

    People are naturally more motivated when they have a reason to do something. With that reason in mind, you will feel more inclined to perform better so you can get the results you seek. A sense of purpose will also fine-tune your focus as you want to get the best results out of your efforts.

- **Address WHEN something needs to be done**

    This one ties in with prioritizing your goals so that important things get done first. Knowing when to do what can make everyday living so much easier to cope with.

    Plus, giving yourself a timeframe to work within helps you stay on task i.e. stay focused so you can then have more time to do the other things you need to do.

Successful time management lets you take control of your life rather than follow others. Plus, you end up accomplishing more, performing better, and becoming more successful at what you do. Added perks include a sense of satisfaction and peace of mind.

But whether it is prioritizing goals, finding a sense of purpose, or practicing time management skills, none of it can be achieved without good focus.

Types of focus

Having established that the ability to focus is a critical element for success in aspects of life, let us now take a look at the different types of focus you need to develop to achieve that success.

Inner focus

This is the most common of all types. Inner focus is an individual's ability to block out distractions, focus on the present moment, task, and stay calm under the pressure. This type of focus develops a person's intuition, gut feeling, and good decision making.

The benefit of establishing inner focus allows you to stay focused on your goals and manage your schedule.

Focusing on others

Not everyone masters this type of focus as it goes beyond what you are doing and demands that you attend to what others are doing and saying instead. This type of focus is especially important in work situations or teamwork scenarios where your output is affected by others' input. However, this type of focus is not only restricted to professional settings but is equally applicable to personal and social contexts as well.

Outer focus

Outer focus goes beyond paying attention to other people and demands paying attention to your surroundings instead. Outer focus is based on peripheral learning and allows a person to think strategically. It also allows for making adjustments to outer surroundings as circumstances around you change.

Chapter 2

Escaping the Busy Trap

Being overwhelmed results in burnout. This produces a condition where the individual feels mentally, emotionally, and physically exhausted. The feeling occurs when you feel overwhelmed and aren't able to keep up with demands. As a result, chaos also factors into the equation and the missing element once again is focus.

The feeling of being persistently overwhelmed can easily cause you to lose interest as well as motivation and bring on a state that leaves you feeling powerless, helpless, and extremely worn out. Once again, you may be trying to do too much- much more than it is realistic to handle.

When talking about burnout, remember that it is not mere exhaustion that you experience. It does not merely affect your performance but every aspect of life. For instance, work may become unbearable, but you will also lose interest in almost everything else that you do. Fun stops being fun while every insignificant thing starts to bother you.

In a state of burnout, this feeling does not go away but sticks around regularly. Staying in this forlorn condition will likely make you believe that there is no alternative or getting out of this mess.

So how do you get yourself out of this rut? You turn your attention to focus.

Remember what being focused taught you in the previous chapter? The WHAT, WHY, and WHEN formula will come in very handy when you feel overwhelmed. Sort out issues by focusing on what's important, figure out why it is so and when to deal with it. Once you have the answers to these simple questions you can at least start to untangle the web of feeling overwhelmed.

Unraveling burnout

However, the problem with feeling overwhelmed is that it is not always possible to identify the burnout yourself. Experts recommend that when feeling distressed, seek out help from friends, family, and others that you trust. They can not only give you an outside opinion but may also be able to help you out by citing examples of why they believe you may be burnt out.

Focus to undo the effects of the burnout

Once you have identified the trigger for your woes, be prepared to make some serious changes. This effort will take a lot of focus on your part as you will not only have to make serious changes but also stick with them for a while. The bright side of this entire episodeis that once you start making the shift, you should also start to feel more motivated again. A good place to start is by focusing and working on some of the following:

- **Cut off the source of the burnout-** Where possible, shun the trigger that is causing you to feel overwhelmed. Job-related burnouts often happen from too many hours working and too little personal time.
- **Try to be healthy-** Being overwhelmed can easily take a toll on health, so engage in some form of physical activity

to give yourself a break. While taking a break may sound counterintuitive to focusing, the idea is to shift the focus from the cause of the burnout and redirect focus on taking care of yourself instead.

- **Eat well-** Focus on taking care of yourself by eating a little better than before. Chances are that being in a burnt-out state, you also neglected your diet. After all, the first thing most people reach for when overwhelmed is an abundance of junk and convenience foods. Chuck these out and refocus on what will make you feel better both on the inside and out.
- **Sleep better-** Last, but not least a burnout will bring forth long term exhaustion with it. The simple coping mechanism for this issue is to focus on getting both good quality and quantity of sleep.

When you want to get out of this despondent state, remember that focus is the one thing holding everything together. It is this ability to concentrate on your wellbeing that will allow you to remove all the negativity out of your life.

The impact of being overwhelmed

While you are in an internal state of being unfocused, things can go horribly wrong in the external world. Personal turbulence aside, the world keeps moving at its pace, continuing to bombard you with the daily grind, moving at a breakneck speed. With decisions and information piling up all the time, it becomes really hard to stay focused. While you may not be able to detect them yourself, certain red flags can identify the most common habits of unfocused people:

- **They don't plan**

    It is very difficult to stay focused without a plan to execute. Unfocused individuals tend to work by whim, rather than by strategy. They seem to get into things that they "think" might be important without really knowing why. On the contrary, people who focus on their goals have a strategy to execute and move progressively through their agenda rather than randomly.

- **They lose track of time**

    If you find yourself running short of time on most of your tasks, you are probably not focusing on good time management. You may be getting too deep into things, where it is not required and end up spending too much time on one specific task which, with focus and planning could have been allotted to multiple tasks instead.

    Being unfocused also makes the individual struggle with keeping track of time.

- **They run late**

    Closely tying in with poor time management is the susceptibility of always running late. Unfocused people not only tend to mismanage time but also exhibit unrealistic ideas about time.

For instance, a common tendency is to have an unclear idea about how long it takes to get to places. It becomes the norm with such people to miscalculate distances or neglect outside factors that may affect travel times.

Another common scenario of being unfocused is when someone takes on a new project without finishing a previous one. The result is nothing but chaos where not many of the projects get done and the individual is left scampering to finish up while running behind on various tasks.

- **They get easily distracted**

    People without focus are the easiest targets of distractions. That is to say that distractions are everywhere; some of them obvious, others not so much, but they do get in the way of getting things done.

    If you are not focused, then every time you switch or shift from one activity to the next, there is a time lag in between. For unfocused folks, this void can easily be filled by sneaky distractions like getting on their cell phone, playing candy crush, and even a simple conversation is enough to take them far away from their assigned task. Does that sound like something that happens to you a lot? If so, you need to work on your focus.

- **They are messy, unorganized and possibly even flaky**

    Being out of focus leaves its mark on the organizational skills of any person. Such people tend to be surrounded by clutter, unable to ever find what they are looking for, and suffer gravely when it comes to productivity.

    They are also unable to follow through on promises, tend to skip out on appointments, and are quite prone to cancel at the last minute.

    Unfocused people have a hard time committing and appear as flaky when they continuously fail to follow through. This not only harms their efforts but can be disastrous for their reputation.

- **They worry about everything**

    If you find that you worry too much or get agitated over every small thing, you need to redirect your focus and channel it on truly important things. Learn to distinguish the substantial stuff from the insubstantial and then focus on that alone.

Chapter 3

Reclaiming Your Time

Now that you know that distraction is the main reason, we lose focus, let us talk a bit about the various forms distractions can take. In many cases, these distractions may not seem as obvious as one imagines but may make you feel scattered or fuzzy instead. The result is that you may end up blaming yourself for not having more control.

At this point, it is important to remember that as we get older, both focus and concentration can change, just as so can memory and other cognitive functions. However, this does not have to be inevitable. On the contrary, certain studies with older individuals reveal that the capacity for strategic learning or decision making may even improve with age.

Certain habits and situations can factor in impairing focus. Most are everyday habits that that be changed with some effort and may become the starting point for you to move ahead with gaining better focus and concentration.

Poor diet and nutrition

Food has a direct impact on cognition which is why a poor decision at lunch can derail an entire afternoon. Why this happens is because everything we eat is converted by the body into glucose providing energy. But not every type of food is processed by the body at the same rate.

So, a poor diet that leads to hunger and dehydration can become a major distraction. Hunger can have a myriad of negative effects on health and behavior including the ability to focus. It is often tied into low blood sugar that directly leads to fatigue, and low energy levels.

Dehydration, on the other hand, can lead to numerous symptoms that can reduce focus including headaches, fatigue and low mood. Studies establish that even 1% lower than optimal hydration can bring about a lack of focus.

So, what are some of the pitfalls you need to avoid to let hunger and dehydration from setting in? Here's a look:

- **Weight loss diets**

    Weight-loss diets are notoriously bad for focus and concentration. Among these low-fat diets can be held accountable as the brain needs essential fatty acids for proper functioning and these fats deprive the body of such nutrients. At the same time, cutting out on important nutrients like proteins is bad as well. This is because the amino acids in protein are essential for optimal brain performance in creating brain chemicals that improve focus.

- **Processed foods**

    Poor nutrition, often in the form of empty calories does not give you the energy that you need. With insufficient energy, the brain has a hard time functioning or focusing on anything properly. As a result, you may find that you experience mild irritability when you eat processed foods.

An example; eating processed foods such as cured meats canmake the brain foggy. When you consume salt and protein-rich foods like these there is a tendency to become dehydrated, and dehydration can diminish cognitive function.

- **Junk foods**

    Junk foods are a whole different story by itself. Junk foods come in a high-fat, high-sugar, and high-calorie package that gets digested fairly quickly. And while you may get instant gratification from eating these foods, they don't do much to satisfy hunger.

    Instead, since junk foods are devoid of nutrients, the body gets forced to engage sugar as a source of energy. This form of energy is quickly spent given the refined nature of sugar, leaving you with a sugar high also experienced as a temporary sensation of energy.

    But after the metabolism has used up all the available energy, the surge is followed by a sugar crash accompanied by a feeling of fatigue, lethargy, focus loss, and a wandering brain.

Hormones at play

Maintaining hormonal equilibrium is key to optimal brain functioning. It may surprise you to know that a deficiency of specific hormones can bring about significant changes in mental focus and processing.

With hormones out of whack, you may find yourself having difficulty remembering people's names, snapping unintentionally, suffering from mood swings, or even start to feel depressed. All these and other factors play a part in affecting the way your brain functions.

For women, the one thing to watch out for is estrogen levels. This female hormone can dictate everything from sugar cravings and bouts of fatigue to mood swings. Any imbalance is then seen as impacting mental agility where low estrogen levels can impair mental functions like memory, reasoning, and even mood from running smoothly.

As a result, women may often observe that fluctuations in estrogen levels during perimenopause and menopause may make their memory and attention wax and wane.

Another consideration that falls under hormonal imbalances and one that can impact the ability to focus is hypothyroidism. Low thyroid issues have been directly linked with causing mental fog, concentration issues, depression, and even short-term memory loss.

An optimal balance of estrogen, progesterone and testosterone must be maintained since all three hormones act directly on nerve cells in the brain. Collectively, these hormones can help facilitate neurotransmission, protect cells from neurotoxins, and improve blood flow in the brain. Any imbalance and the result could be a significant drop in cognition, mental focus, and the ability to sustain concentration.

Lack of sleep

This common issue does not get the true attention it deserves. Even with a single night of insufficient sleep, the mind suffers greatly and focus becomes compromised. When you don't sleep well, your thought processes slow down, and you become less alert. This affects your ability to concentrate and can make the mind confused enough to prevent you from performing tasks that require complex thought.

Also, feeling sleepy can cut into your working memory which is an important component of focusing. The sensation makes you less vigilant and reduces the speed and accuracy of mental tasks.

Stress

While memory and cognitive functioning gradually diminish with age, people with persistent or higher levels of stress are especially vulnerable. The negative effects of stress on memory can cause the brain to freeze and completely lose track of focus. This can happen in any scenario from students studying for an exam to introducing a friend and forgetting their name mid-way through introductions.

Focus caves in to stress in these situations as thinking gets preoccupied with stress-inducing stimuli that other thoughts fail to emerge. In this way, it hampers working memory which is associated with short term memory.

Lack of physical activity

Regular exercise releases brain chemicals which are key for memory and a lack of the same can impact focus and concentration. Exercise stimulates areas of the brain which are involved in memory functions. Physical activity releases a chemical called BDNF or brain-derived neurotrophic factor which rewires memory circuits so they work better.

As such 30 minutes of exercise can help make more BNDF. But doing so once a week won't help. Exercise needs to be made a regular part of daily routine to reap cognitive benefits.

Surrounding environment

The environment where you are sitting down can quickly become a distracting factor when you are trying to concentrate. There could be multiple diversions such as loud noises, bright lighting, visual disruptions, and even temperature inconsistencies.

Even though they may seem trivial, these environmental variables can play an important role in making or breaking focus.

Quality of information

Another common distraction is the quality of information you need to process. If the information is relevant to the task at hand, then it will likely keep your focus engaged but you can easily become distracted if you don't have the right information to work with. Issues like an incomplete email, a skipped step, or a misleading phone message can mess up your focus as you try to make sense of the situation.

Chapter 4

Benefits of Being Focused

So far it is safe to say that being focused can help yield great benefits not only for the mind and body but the overall life quality of a person. Here is how being focused can help you achieve greater success and control of your life:

Helps take control

When you are focused, you can take control of the things that you are doing. But if you are not focused, that task or thing will end up controlling you. Once you become focused on something and you have channeled all your energy into that particular task, you can handle the task in a better way.

Control will also come easy when you apply all the three types of focus simultaneously into all your tasks. Inner focus will keep you on track and away from distractions while paying attention to others makes you more aware. But it is perhaps outer focus that will be most beneficial in gaining control since it gives you the flexibility to give you a contingency plan if needed.

Yields positive energy

Being focused helps harvest positive energy in the body. It also allows you to get yourself out of a negative spiral and put things into perspective.

When you look at different aspects of daily life, the instinctive reaction is to pay attention to the deficits and focus on what's wrong.

Because attention amplifies everything, focusing on the negative aspects will make everything worse. Instead, it is best to detach from the problem and reinvest focus on how to make the best out of a bad situation.

Everyday obstacles are an unavoidable occurrence, but when you focus on the positive it can help you get through difficult times more steadily.

Perhaps scenarios like this will demand that you bring out your inner focus fully since such situations affect the individual personally. The same can also create chaos in life, so focusing on the positive can help reduce or get rid of this chaos completely.

Enhances problem-solving skills

One of the most important benefits of staying focused is that it refines your problem-solving skills. If you are not focused, you will never make it through a problem.

The way an individual approaches a problem can vary greatly. For instance, one person may focus more on the reason the problem exists, rather than the solution, and the other vice versa. The former of these will have *problem-focused thinking* while the latter will engage in *solution-focused thinking*.

Of the two, problem-focused thinking will not help solve anything but solution-focused thinking can yield the opposite result.

Instills decision-making skills

The ability to make decisions is crucial for survival and cannot be executed without focus. Successful decision making is based on the principles of logical and critical thinking which need to be focus based. Whether you are a boss or an employee, whether you are a parent or a student, you need to make several decisions either on a daily basis or on an occasional basis. None of the decisions can be made until and unless you are completely focused on the issue.

Additionally, the issue does not resolve by simply making any decision, but it has to be the right one. Plus making the right decision also involves executing it correctly. The process includes identifying critical decisions and filtering out unimportant ones.

Making the right decision also means you need to focus on getting the right information to make a good decision.

Removes distractions

Success is not something that can be achieved without determination and will power. To have both these attributes, you need to focus on getting rid of distractions.

While it may seem that people who are highly organized and successful are just like everybody, this is not the case. Instead, they have several habits that are associated with the elimination of distractions from their life.

Distractions can take you away from your goals and aims. Even on daily basis, even the most common distraction can make the completion of the task an impossibility. Thus, you need to stay focused because it is only through staying focused that you can succeed in getting rid of distractions.

Once you can do that, nothing is stopping you from achieving your goals or getting your tasks done. At the end of the day, it always comes down to how focused you are on your goal. If you ask any famous and successful person, you would see that focus was a big part of their story. It's because what you constantly focus on will eventually become your reality.

Gets things done

This is probably the one benefit of being focused that we all feel in our daily life. If you stay focused, there is a better chance of you being able to finish something you started or complete something that you are supposed to do. Anyone who is not focused, tends to postpone the task to some next day or another time and as a result, the task remains undone. Being focused is the demand of every profession and every field of life. In every single sphere of life, you will need to be focused to get done what needs to get done.

Generates satisfaction

Staying focused also makes you feel content with yourself and everyone else around you. If you are not focused on one thing and your mind is always wandering around, you will have more pressure and stress on your mind and body. This robs you of any peace that you could hope for.

When you're focused, you can just keep one thing in front of your eyes and work on it diligently. Your brain and body will be in sync with what you need to accomplish at that given time.

Builds momentum

Focus increases effectiveness which in turn lets you progress faster with your tasks. The faster you get your scheduled tasks out of the way, the greater your productivity.

Focus based momentum also helps you stay on track and prevents derailing. On the other hand, changing direction deflates momentum and disturbs focus as well. This point can also tie in with multitasking where you may be trying to get too much done at one time, and every task suffers. So, to stay in momentum, start a job on time, finish it all the way through and then move on to the next task.

Reduces stress

Staying focused also helps reduce stress as all your concentration will be on the task at hand. A lack of focus, on the other hand, leads to becoming overwhelmed with too much to do and too little time.

Being overwhelmed also impairs your judgment on where to start and that can be stressful too. With focus, clarity becomes improved, allows you to get out of being overwhelmed which, in turn, reduces stress and leads to improved outcomes.

With clarity intact, you can see the progress you are making and will work with focus to achieve your desired results.

Increases engagement

Focus gives direction and purpose to a task. In this sense, it engages the interest and effort of the individual. With a clear-cut target in sight, you will not be hesitant to put in additional effort, since most people are not afraid of hard work but the possibility of failure.

When goals are not articulated, it becomes hard and even impossible to focus on how to achieve them. Focus-oriented direction will pique interest and engagement in all scenarios.

Chapter 5

How Highly Successful People Develop Self-Discipline

What most people have in common with successful people is ambition, but where certain individuals fall short, and others excel, is in the area of self-discipline.

According to Dennis Prager, "Happiness is dependent on self- discipline." The biggest hurdle in achieving our goals is how easily we let ourselves be distracted by things that do not count as progress towards our achievements.

However, practicing self-discipline is not easy and demands real commitment. To develop self-discipline, you must follow certain steps that will help you attain your goals. Here are the top habits of successful people that help that maintain self-discipline which ultimately helps them achieve their goals:

Vision

Highly successful people know exactly where they want to be in life. They know exactly where you want to go. It is impossible to be successful without knowing where you want to be.

To be successful, create a vision board. Curate pictures and quotes that motivate you to achieve what you want to and look at it before you start your day. This will help you align your tasks with your goals. To visualize, you must have a conscious purposefulness which helps you in clearing up your headspace.

Prioritize

Another thing about self-disciplined people is that they finish their important tasks before they allow themselves any indulgences.

It is very important to prioritize everything so that you face less distractions during your day. Getting important tasks done first relieves the pressure of an undone task and also gives you plenty of time to be productive for the rest of the day.

For instance, if working on your next project will help you be successful in the future, then it is important you work on it before you let yourself spend time with friends, on your phone, etc. As the saying goes, "Being lazy is the best reward for finishing tasks now."

Say no to distractions

The strongest habit of highly successful people is their courage to say no to distractions. Successful people are just as prone to get distracted by social media and hangouts as you but they square up and say "no" to work toward their goals. This does not mean you can never indulge in social media presence or go out with friends but prioritizing your work is important.

Many people lack the courage to say no to hanging out when they know they should be working. Once you have learned to say you will notice that you are moving towards your goals. It is so easy to get distracted by people who are chilling but "Don't get distracted by people who are not on track."

Handle one task at a time

Highly successful people are realistic with their to-do lists. If you have spent a lot of your days procrastinating then it is impossible to suddenly finish everything in a day. Start by trying to focus on one task at a time instead of overwhelming yourself with the thought of everything that is not finished.

"If the finish line feels too far away, don't look at it." Keep yourself focused on what you have at hand and make sure that you do your best while you are at it.

Divide up goals

Once you have a bigger goal in mind, you must divide it in smaller chunks. You need to know all the steps that you must take to achieve what you want. Instead of moping around, get realistic. Divide your goal into what needs to be done each day, each week, each month or in six months.

"A goal without a plan is just a wish." You cannot expect everything you want to magically appear in front of you. It takes hard work and every successful person in history put that hard work in to turn their dreams into reality.

Rewards and breaks

You cannot stay focused unless you give yourself sufficient breaks during the day. Every business, school, or workplace, have breaks after a certain period because the body cannot function continuously for so long without resting. If you want to keep distractions at bay, it is essential to take breaks during the day or working period.

You must acknowledge your hard work because your mind is more likely to stay focused on goals when you give it breaks. Otherwise, you will physically and mentally feel overwhelmed and burn yourself out.

After each day of doing what you intended to, reward yourself with an hour of social media, dinner with friends, or just staying in and chilling on your own. This will also energize you and motivate you to work the next day.

Make sure that you take one day each week where you don't do anything. This is important to give you a break before you start working again.

Learn from mistakes

Another thing that highly successful people do is learn from their mistakes instead of quitting. So, what if you made a mistake? It only adds to your experience and teaches you how to maneuver things better.

Every time you make a mistake, remind yourself that it is a blessing. The more mistakes you make the more you take yourself on the right path. Every goal is an accumulation of lessons that you learned from your mistakes along the way.

Rise above feelings

When we know what we need to do our feelings can be contagious and deceptive. We can make ourselves believe that we can take a break after one day of working hard or two days of working hard. Consistency is the key to achievement.

Don't argue with the plan you have made for yourself. It is only habitual to deny hard work because we become accustomed to laziness. If you want to achieve something don't be passive to feelings that lead to the destruction of your plan.

You will have plenty of time for laziness, self-pity and fatigue when you are done with your tasks.

Love what you do

You must look at hard work as a positive trait rather than something that strains you. When we force ourselves to work hard it is natural to hate it because we cannot waste time anymore. Successful people love their work and therefore it is easier for them to put in the effort that is needed to achieve their goals.

Whenever you feel distressed because of all that you need to get done, remind yourself why you are doing it in the first place. This will help you develop a positive mindset towards your work.

Manipulate energy

Self-disciplined people do not burn themselves out. Instead, they devote their effort to tasks that need energy. Sometimes people make the mistake of building up all their energy for a task that does not need as much energy and later they feel tired or fatigued because they used it all up.

To achieve your goals, know what demands your active motivation, and what you can do without using effort. This is a difficult task for those who are starting from zero therefore start by taking up one task and perfecting it until it becomes a habit.

Then add another and slowly build up to it. "Relax but don't get too comfortable." Your mind will fool you into believing that you have done a lot when you achieve one goal but it is not always true.

In a nutshell, you can keep reading tips on self-discipline but the real effort is to apply them in real life. Instead of looking around for more tips, start practicing them now.

As perhaps one of his most famous quotes, Steve Jobs said, "If today were the last day of your life, would you want to do what you are about to do?"

Always look ahead to the future. If you dream of success then it is time to push away all your distractions and start working on your goals.

Chapter 6

Strategies to Building Unbreakable Focus

Whether you are a student, a parent, or a worker, you are aware of the importance of focus for everything that you do in your life. Whether there is a short-term plan to follow, or a long-term goal neither can be accomplished without focus.

There are a few strategies that you can use to build an unbreakable focus. Once you succeed in making these strategies a part of your life, you will be much more in touch with yourself and you will experience a self of accomplishment that nothing else can give you.

Train your brain

This is the most essential part of the focus building process. Your brain controls everything that goes on in your body. Whether it is something you think, something you see, or something that you feel, everything is controlled by your brain. This is why you need to have extensive control over your brain and you need to train it to stay focused.

Make a habit of repeating the task at hand, to yourself again and again. Prepare yourself mentally for what you are about to do. Before you do anything, sit in a quiet place and let it sink into your brain that you are going to spend the next few hours on a specific task. This is a mind strengthening exercise that you need to do to keep focused. If you train your brain well enough, it will not be sidetracked by any distractions after that.

Plan it all out

Before you start anything, you need to plan it all out. This does not only apply to everyday tasks but it also applies to long term tasks. For example, businesses that tend to have a business plan for a year or a semester have a better chance of increasing sales and making a mark. When you plan something, you lay all the tasks out in front of you.

This makes it easier for you to determine which things require your utmost attention. Using this plan, you can also schedule the time for the completion of your task and you can divide every task of yours into time intervals.

When you know that you have to finish a particular task in a given time frame, you will be able to maintain your focus better.

Rest for a while

The human body is not made for functioning constantly, which is why the concept of sleep is present in the body. No matter how much work needs to be done, you need to rest for a while. Take a half an hour break after every 4 or 5 hours that you work. This would help to freshen up your brain and it will also give you time to relax. During this time, you can clear your brain and simply give time to yourself.

By resting or taking breaks, you can quickly build up focus. This strategy has proven to be successful even by scientific methods.

Workplaces have a lunch break and other breaks during the day so that employees can stay productive for the whole day. This is particularly important if you are doing an extensive activity. It becomes harder to focus so you need to give your brain and body a break. In these few minutes or half an hour, do what soothes your body. Listen to calming music or simply go for a walk in some calm neighborhood.

Work with music

This strategy may not work with everyone but it has shown to be successful in most cases. Listening to music is something most people enjoy. You could try by playing your favorite music in the background while you work. It is better if the song is not too loud because that can cause distraction.

The music must not be too loud to distract you from the work that you are doing. However, people who are prone to dancing around with their favorite music may not benefit from this strategy as much.

Practice mindfulness

Using mindfulness to build focus is probably one of the best techniques. The key step involved is to sit in a quiet place and take a deep breath in. After that, you are required to hold your breath for a few seconds and then exhale. It is during this pause that you need to bring your mind back to the thing that it needs to be on.

Your mind tends to drift away every once in a while, because the lifespan of human concentration is merely 8 seconds. It is due to this reason that you need to make this exercise a habit so that you can benefit from it. It also serves as a reliever of stress and can rid the body of any negative energy. Once you harbor positiveenergy in the body and you shift your brain's function to one task, your focus will automatically improve.

Since we are all creatures of habit, integrating the right habits into your workday will help immensely. Once something becomes a habit, it also becomes easy. If focusing becomes a habit, it will come to you naturally and will let you have multiple benefits daily.

Limit phone usage

A major distraction for many people is cell phone usage and portable technology. It can easily distract you from the task that you are supposed to do.

Most students can relate to situations where they have assignments or pending projects but instead, they are busy on their cellphones.

So, while you are working, make sure that you put your phone away to avoid being distracted by incoming calls or messages. If you work on your phone, install an app that lets you block notifications from social media sites.

In instances where you do not have any specific work to do on the phone, there can still be an inclination to use it for social media.

This is another thing that can distract you from your task and ultimately your goals.

Set a time for using your phone. Sometime in the evening or after dinner is a good timeslot for this type of activity. Most people are done with their day's work by dinner time and may use their phones as much as they want.

Give constant reminders

Another way to get rid of distractions is to constantly remind yourself about your goals and aims that you hope to accomplish. Once you do that, you will be inclined towards doing what you need to do instead of wasting your time on unnecessary things.

Any businessperson or individual hoping to make a mark constantly reminds himself of the goal he is hoping to achieve. A daily reminder first thing in the morning is a good place to start.

Plan your day

Another way to keep distractions away is to plan your day. When you go to bed, make a habit to make a little plan for the next day in your mind. Keep the unnecessary things out of it and make sure that you sort out the things according to the amount of time you have on your hands and the task that needs to be done first.

When you do so, your brain will slowly be trained to only pay attention to the tasks that you have planned for that day. It is also useful to have a planner or a diary that you can keep with you. People who have a diary are more organized and they tend to get more work done on time.

When you make this a habit, you will be able to stick to your schedule. It is the hardest to not deviate from the plan but with practice, it can become second nature. This habit can lead to success and your brain will automatically cancel out any task it finds unnecessary that is, any task not mentioned in the plan.

Having positive energy is very important as it energizes the body for functioning in the best way possible.

Brain Updates

Your brain is like a computer. It does it updates and works on problems in the background at night…if you tell it to before you sleep. It's like a genie in the bottle, your wish, is actually your command. But what about the rest of the day? One focus strategy is to understand when your brain can focus the best and then use that time to work on your most difficult tasks. The average person finds that time to be between 10AM and noon. Before that, your brain is still gearing up and not running at full capacity. After lunch, the brain typically starts to wind down but can still focus on items. It can be charged up by taking a walk, meditating, or a power nap but it still won't be at peak performance as it is at 10AM.

Enthusiasm

When you have very little enthusiasm for the task at hand, ask yourself if this should be shifted to a different time. Let's say it is 3PM and you try to work but drift into a daydream about that Porsche you always wanted. No matter what you do to come back around, you drift. Ask yourself if you can put this task aside and pick one that you know will crank you up. If so, take the other task and reschedule it for 10 am the next morning, when you will have much more control over your focus.

Water

Always have an abundant supply of water and fruit/raw vegetables on the corner of your desk. As you are working, your brain may start to try and wander, first by saying you're tired. Then it tries the old, you must be thirsty or hungry trick. By having water, you can stop this tactic in its tracks. The water will refresh and rehydrate you. Having healthy snacks right there, means you don't lose focus by getting up and going in search of something to eat in the café or the local convenience store ten minutes down the road.

Cleanliness

Keep your desk clear at all times. Start with a quick tidy up in the morning and before you leave for the day. Clutter plays havoc with your ability to focus on a task. You try to work on a task and cannot find your favorite pen or the notes you made last night are now lost under a pile of paperwork. When this happens, it gives you an excuse to head off to the coffee shop for coffee and a cookie.

Theme

Pick a theme for your day. This is like a bit of method acting and how it helps with overall focus, is by forcing you to focus on one theme. So, what are themes? Well, there are self-confidence, humility, and integrity, for starters.

Do you find that you are not the most self-confident person in your office? Use the self-confidence theme starting on a Monday. As soon as you walk through the door, focus on being self-confident in the way you talk to co-workers or your supervisor. As you tackle your biggest, toughest task at 10AM, start by repeating how confident you are that you can crush this task at a ten out of ten. Do a few Tony Robbins fist pumps and say, "yeah, I got this!" Themes will help you focus better and increase your personal growth.

Rhythm

Now that you have made it through the day and have been focused and self-confident, it is time for home and later for bed. Proper sleep is essential for focus and the body is tuned into what is called the "Circadian Rhythm." This is the body's natural sleep pattern and it is optimum at 8 hours of sleep, best done between 10PM and 6AM. Not everyone can meet these hours, so adjust accordingly. The least you should sleep for best performance and focus is 6 hours a night.

Chapter 7

Why Should You Focus on One Thing at A Time

Multitasking is trying to split focus and divide your attention to getting multiple projects done at a time. While many believe that this practice gets more done, that may not always be the case. Instead, while trying to increase the quantity of jobs being performed, you may well be compromising the quality of every one of them.

The result is hurting your productivity while shifting focus from one task to the other without being fully attentive to any single one. Instead, here is a look at why you should only focus on one thing at a time.

It gets things done

The best part about doing one thing at a time is that it gets things done. When you focus all your attention and your energy on one thing, you ensure that the particular task will get done and it will be done on time. For you to accomplish any task, you need to have excessive focus. The thing about focus is that it gets diverted easily if there are more things on your mind.

When you are doing one thing at a time, your focus is only on that one task and it gets done promptly. On the contrary, if you try to do three things at the same time, then your focus will be divided between them and you will not be able to do any single one of them.

It leaves less room for error

Everyone who does more than one thing at a single time knows that there is a much greater chance of error when you are doing so. On the other hand, when you give your undivided attention to one thing only, you can do it with much more accuracy. Multitasking is switching between tasks, and when it boils down to concentration and productivity, the brain only has a limited amount.

A common example is people using their cell phones while driving. Since you are not focusing on one thing only, there is a huge margin for error. Even in less impacting issues such as texting, this phenomenon can be seen. If you text four or five people at the same time, there is a likelihood that you will end up sending the wrong thing to the wrong person. It is due to this reason that you need to keep your focus on one thing only.

The accomplishment of tasks should not be your only goal. Your goal should be to do the task in the best way possible with minimum error. To make this possible, it is essential to stay focused on one thing at a single time and not have a lot of different things to do at the same time.

Higher success rate

If you focus on one thing at a time, you end up having a better chance of succeeding at something. This is not only applicable in the case of businesses or entrepreneurs, but also in everyday situations. People who try to do only one thing at a time are more likely to be attentive as well than those who try to do everything at the same time.

In the same way, the probability of being successful is higher if you focus on one thing at a time. Businesses tend to focus on one thing for the time being, such as making their marketing more efficient or increasing employee productivity instead of trying to do all of these things at once. It is not possible to juggle so many things at once so the better approach is to take one step at a time.

It does not deplete energy

If you have a habit of doing many things at one time, you will always be tired and will suffer from a lack of energy. This is why it is better to focus on one thing instead of trying to go for three or four things.

The human brain may be like a machine when it comes to its functionality but it has the human character of tiredness.

It gets tired after long hours of activity or after doing many things at the same time. When you try to do a lot of things at the same time, you are putting a lot of strain on the brain. As a result of this, the energy reserves of the body are exploited which leads to a decrease in the energy levels of the body.

You might feel that you are capable of doing many things at the same time but the truth is that the internal functioning of your body is not entirely invisible to you. So, you cannot know how an activity is harming the inside of your body.

If you focus on one thing at a time, you can direct your brain to do the same thing for a precise period. When your brain only has to accomplish one task at a time, it can function more effectively. However, if you are trying to cook, clean, and write an essay at the same time, the brain and body are going to have a hard time trying to keep up with the levels of your activity.

If your work involves physical work, it can also tire out your body and when the body is not active, there is no way you can focus on a task to make it more successful. When your glucose levels run out, your body function also decreases.

It keeps distractions away

Another benefit of doing one thing at a time is that it keeps distractions at bay. When you try to do more than one task at a time, you will find your brain wandering off to the other task that needs to be done. Using the example mentioned above, if you are trying to cook but your brain is constantly focused on the content you need for your essay, it is not unlikely that you will be successful in any of your tasks.

You may be able to cook and finish your essay but the essay is not going to be the best you have ever written and the cooking is not going to be satisfactory. When you focus all your attention and concentration on one thing, you can easily accomplish your task as your brain is only thinking of the current task at hand.

It lets you enjoy work

Let's admit it. If you are trying to juggle too many things at the same time, you will not be able to enjoy any of it. Just imagine writing emails while having dinner. There is no way you are going to enjoy your dinner due to the distraction and it is also probable that you will end up making mistakes in your emails.

Similarly, at work or during studying, if you do not focus on one thing at a time, you will not be able to enjoy it. Most people do not enjoy their work because they are trying to manage a whole lot of tasks at once. When you start doing one thing at a time, you will find the process more enjoyable and easier to accomplish.

Conclusively, multitasking can prove to be pretty unproductive as lower quality work is unproduced, more mistakes are made and both time and effort get wasted.

Chapter 8

Online Tools for Laser Focus

The hardest thing for most people is to live in the present moment. It has become difficult to stay focused on one task with so many distractions around us. But this type of lifestyle also affects our efficiency at the workplace as our mind wanders and we struggle to finish our tasks on time.

However, while the internet has provided us with multiple distractions in form of social media it has also generated tools that can be help organize, and finish tasks on time. Here is a list of some applications that will help you regain your laser focus and control your time instead of letting internet distractions control it:

1. Stayfocused

StayFocused is an extension that works on Chrome. There are many ad blockers or website blockers that can be added to Chrome. However, this one is designed to help you get work done instead of spending hours on Twitter or Facebook. You can also set break times which means you can set time where you will be allowed to enter websites but as soon as your break time is over you will not be allowed to enter them again.

The "Nuclear Option" is for those who absolutely cannot resist their distractions. This will not let you enter any of the websites that keep you from working and it cannot be deactivated until after the provided time.

2. Freedom

This is an application for web, pc, iOS and Mac that can be installed to block out websites that distract you so you can pay attention to what needs to be done. Making to-do lists is fun but getting everything done on your to-do list is a challenge when you have a habit of spending hours scrolling through your favorite social media.

Freedom lets you manage schedules so you can block certain websites for a certain time. For instance, if you spend hours scrolling through Facebook, you can add it on the Freedom app to block it from 9:00 AM to 2:00 PM while you finish your work. Freedom will not let you enter the land of distraction within the scheduled time.

It also has a "Locked Mode" which can be turned on to prevent from breaking the given schedule and giving in to your craving for social media. When you have a habit of procrastination, it is impossible to avoid going back to that lifestyle but with locked mode you can easily avoid it.

3. FocusWriter

This application is for those whose work requires a lot of writing. However, many writers struggle with focusing on their writing while working on their laptops. If you also struggle with staying focused on your work then this is a great website that pops-up a plain grey background to write on and everything else is blocked away including timer and date until your scheduled time is over.

FocusWriter also includes features like word count and spell- check which are crucial to writing jobs and assignments. It also has certain other features like setting a writing goal which will bring gratification once you have achieved your goal. Besides that, the typewriting sounds with each key make it interesting to work with FocusWriter.

4. Concentrate

This application is designed to manage different types of tasks. Sometimes people can start their day intensely motivated to get everything done but after one task they tend to get distracted before they can start the next task. Concentrate will block out the email client and browser to keep you away from Buzzfeed, YouTube, Twitter, etc. while you are writing. Launch applications feature allows you to access only the applications that are needed for tasks in hand.

The "Speak a Message" feature allows you to record a message that will play at a set time and motivate you to concentrate on your work. This Mac application is designed to help you stick to your schedule for the day until you have finished everything.

5. Be Focused

Be Focused application uses Pomodro technique because it has been proven that people tend to focus on their tasks better if they take breaks in between. Many people struggle to take a break from fear of losing attention but they end up losing focus with time. Be Focused will give you short breaks after 25 minutes of working and longer intervals before you switch from one task to another.

You can create a list of tasks and track your progress as you move along. This iOS application is perfect if you don't want to lose enthusiasm as you progress. You will get time to rejuvenate your headspace and be ready to take up the next task efficiently.

6. Forest

If you feel like your phone is chained to your hands and keep you from working then Forest app will help you leave it be while you finish your work. This is an interesting application that allows you to grow a forest. Whenever you activate it, you plant a tree and the tree will die if you interrupt or deactivate.

Forest application has partnered with Trees for the Future and every tree you make, is being planted in the world. This means that each tree you plant will earn you virtual coins which will be spent on plantation of trees.

7. Hold

Hold is an application that is specially designed for students and keeps an eye on their activity. If you struggle with studying or finish your papers because you cannot resist Instagram feed and Facebook comments then this application is for you. For every 20 minutes that you spend away from your phone, you earn a point.

When you have earned fifteen points you get a reward in the shape of raffle tickets or coffee from 7-eleven. Many students who have used this application testified that their grades improved by using the Hold app.

8. Noisli

Some people tend to focus better on their application when they are surrounded by an ideal ambiance. Noisli provides ambient noises like the seaside, bonfire crackles, a fan, etc. so you can customize a combination of your favorite sounds so you can have the perfect atmosphere to work in.

Noisli is therefore an application for those who want to work in a particular environment which will help them stay focused on the task. Noisli also has another feature inspired by Pomodro techniques which helps you divide your tasks and Chromotherapy inspired feature lets you choose a certain background color while you work.

9. Balanced

Balanced is an application that helps you build your focus by creating a balance in your life. You must maintain a healthy lifestyle that consists of reading, meditation, workout, walking, etc. Balanced tracks your time spent on doing things that you wish you did more.

Some people struggle with reading books while others cannot stay focused on yoga. Balanced will keep you motivated to include these tasks in your daily life and stay focused on them.

10. Hocus Focus

Hocus Focus is another application made to improve your productivity by making your browser tab clutter-free. It is no secret that we tend to focus better when we have a cleaner environment. The same is true about working on your PC.

Hocus Pocus will close any website that you are not actively using. For instance, if you have distracting applications like Twitter, Buzzfeed, Facebook, etc. open in the background then they will shut off while you start working. Research shows that it takes 23 minutes for an average human brain to refocus and a distracting application can make it even harder.

Bonus 1

Focus Checklists to Get You Started

Focus for Students

1. Practice belly breathing to learn how to focus all the attention on one spot.

2. Set aside time to learn to focus.

3. Commit to one area of study only.

4. Always study in the same place. Have a quiet area set aside with good lighting.

5. Have a timed study with focus and always take scheduled breaks for water and stretching.

Focus for Busy Moms

1. Plan your hardest daily tasks when the child is scheduled for naps or has scheduled television time.

2. Put time limits on tasks. Instead of trying to clean the house for two hours and watch your children, do the household tasks in time blocks as permitted.

3. Visualize first thing in the morning what your day will consist of and make the pictures in your head, happy, and focused on a great day.

3. Be honest with your kids. If you need time to yourself or time to complete a task tell them the truth and ask for their cooperation.

5. Being a stay at home parent is rewarding but hard work. Make sure you eat properly, lots of water, veggies, and fruit throughout the day and then a healthy dinner.

Focus for Working at Home

1. Pick a style of music that energizes you and helps you focus on your project.

2. When you lose sight of what you want to accomplish, take a doodle break. Grab a pencil and let the pictures or words free flow onto the paper.

3. Unplug the computer from the internet if any type of writing is involved and just use a word document. Some find it useful to buy a 2nd computer that does not have all the extras and do their writing on that while being unplugged from the internet.

4. Lighten the mood when you find it just isn't flowing. Bouncing a small rubber ball or just get up and dance like a manic. Get yourself smiling.

5. Build a vision board and during a few rest breaks, gaze at your board and focus on your dreams, what you need, and want in your life.

Focus for Creative People

1. Creative people tend to focus better in dimmer lighting. Experiment with the lighting and the temperature to see what puts you at your peak.

2. Creative people can use music to focus on new ideas. Background music like waves crashing on the rocks, with seagulls in the background is one idea. If that is not to your taste, try instrumental new wave.

3. Play around with your desk and the type of chair you use. Give one of those big round balls you can sit on a try or move to the office couch and put up your feet while using the laptop.

4. Schedule a group chat for ten minutes to bounce ideas off each other, no matter how crazy they are. Focus on the ones that will spark new ideas.

5. Get a Yoga lunch group together. Drink your water and release tension while gaining focus on what you want to accomplish in your day.

Focus at Work

1. Get your coffee or tea ready at the start of your workday. Put your water and healthy snacks over on the other corner of your desk.

2. While drinking your caffeine beverage focus on what might cause a distraction during your work day and make a plan to eliminate it before it starts.

3. Have the desk, nice and tidy, with a short to-do list posted above your desk. Ask yourself if you can work offline today and do that if you can to avoid emails, social media, or checking the news.

4. Get the boss on board with focus and productivity. Ask what they will allow for you to focus. Can you work with your door closed, wear headphones at your station with the rule in place…door closed or headphones on means no (interruptions?)

5. Decide what focus apps you will use at work and make sure they are downloaded and working before starting your day. You can get focus apps for your computer, android, or iPhone that will keep you on track.

Bonus 2

21 Day Focus Challenge

Taking action is the hardest part for the majority of people. They know, or at least have a good idea of what they want to do, but the idea of just getting started can tend to overwhelm them.

The 21 Day Focus Challenge is designed to lift you and help you clear that hurdle with room to spare.

For the next 21 days, you will receive an action step. Some of the action steps have sub-components and will be carried over to the next day for you to continue working on them.

The reason for not putting a huge action step into a single day challenge is simple. Just looking at a huge action step, will stop a lot of people in their tracks. We don't want you to stop. It is essential that you do each challenge, every day and they are designed in a way, that it should take you between 20 to 40 minutes, each and every day.

At the end of 21 days, you will have taken massive action and be fully focused on what you need to do in order to have a laser focus on all areas of your life.

There are two ways to complete this challenge. The best way is to edit this document and type your answers out under each section. You can then go back and read over what you have written and edit, or come up with new ideas down the road.

Nothing is set in concrete, so you should be ready to change and adapt. The second way is to get a decent size notebook and write your answers in that. However, this means you would need to refer back to this document, to refresh your mind as to what each action step was. In this challenge for simplicity, we will just say "write in your notebook."

Get ready to start the pathway to being completely focused.

Day 1-Step up your success by writing the statement highlighted below, at least 25 times, if not more. You need to memorize this statement because you are going to repeat it every night before you sleep.

> **"I release all negative energy from my body and mind. I command my subconscious mind to bring me laser focus on all that I do."**

There is a two-part reason why you need to do this. First up, many people find it difficult to sleep at night, and take over 30 minutes to finally fall into a restless sleep. Great sleep is essential for focus. By repeating the phrase over and over until you drift off, you keep your mind from replaying negative events from the day.

Second, your brain will do as you command, when you command it. Most people allow their brain to wander here and there and repeat negative issues. This happens because your subconscious mind believes that since you think negative, that is what you want, so it gives you more of what you ask for.

Constantly repeating the phrase every night will cue your brain to search and bring into action what you desire. The ability to focus on what truly matters will become much easier and shortly become a part of your daily life.

Day 2-Grab a fresh notebook or open a new word document and title it, "21 Focus Challenge." Think about your ability to laser focus on 1 task for 20-30 minutes before taking a 5-minute break. Then another burst of 20-30 minutes on the same task. Rate yourself on a scale of 1-10. If you are having a hard time rating yourself, then picture the last major big task you did for work. Think about how long you worked on it before taking a break, answering a call, or checking Facebook.

Now give yourself a rating. Write down everything that caused you to lose focus. Total it up and circle it.

You need to decrease the amount of disruptions to your tasks, so circling it, you can come back later and see how you are progressing. Look at your lost focus and decide how to reverse that area. Write down the steps you can take.

Day 3-Now we make a list of personal and business. In separate columns, put down, "relationships, health and fitness, business and finance. If you have others, that is fine put those down too. Under each column, think about how well you focus in those areas and again, write down where you stand on a scale of one to ten.

The area with the lowest score is the one you need to fix first. If your finances score is four of ten for example...this is going to have a major impact on your relationship and your mental health. Let's get that up to a ten out ten. Next time, we will look at each area individually and give you some help on getting results

Day 4-What are you passionate about? Here we ask the question… are we doing something we would do, even if we didn't get paid? You can focus on a job that you don't like or are neutral about, but it is much harder. The average person would prefer to do a job that they are passionate about.

It's time to write down what you are passionate about and how you could make a living doing it.

You might even boost your income while staying at your old job, while you evaluate the success of the passionate job. Make a list now. Write down your current job and then the careers you think that you could be passionate about.

Then beside each one, rate them on a scale of one to ten. Which job could you focus 100% on? If your current job is rated four out of ten and you have a passion for organizing your space and all your families and friends, that is rated eight out of ten-then it's time to revisit your life goals. Determine where you want to put your focus and achieve happiness.

Day 5-Relationships. What you can do to focus on your significant other and improve your relationship? This is super important. If you are not putting a great deal of focus into your relationship, everything else is going to suffer too.

Know of anyone in a bad relationship, that can focus on their job and excel? There are not many people that can do that. It's hard to get up and at it, when you went to bed angry at your significant other.

Rate your current relationship with your significant other on our usual scale. How happy are you with your rating? If you are feeling discomfort, then that means you have some work to do. List the items that make you unhappy with your partner. Then list out what you believe your partner would put in their list.

These are the items you need to focus on. For instance, in your list, if you wrote down that your partner spends four to five hours a night watching television, while you cannot focus that long on poor quality programming, then something has to change.

Work on getting your partner to cut down on viewing time and pick something that you can both engage in.

In your partner's list, you wrote that you have your cellphone in your hand constantly and this is something they talk about, it's time to change. Visit the reason why you are always checking your phone.

Is it serious business or randomly checking to see who is upset with who on Facebook. Find the time to put your cellphone in another room and then focus on your partner and engage in meaningful conversation.

Day 6-External family, friends, and co-workers, for the most part, are cooperative and not negative. To be clear, external family means we are talking about someone other than a spouse or your children. This could be a brother, uncle. or niece.

There is usually one or perhaps two that do not add value to your life. Focus on improving relations with those who are borderline and consider removing those who will continue to hurt your focus and energy. Take the time to make three lists.

<u>External</u> <u>family-Friends-Coworkers</u>

Use your scale out of ten to rate each person on the three lists. Now find the low scoring ones. Those would be the ones who cause you to lose focus by impacting you with negative words or actions. They might demand your time because they want to offload their work onto yours.

Everyone has a relative who constantly needs a drive or wants their kids picked up by someone else. Friends who day in and day bombard you with the story of how their significant other is ruining their life.

How about co-workers, who drop a file on your desk and then tell you a sad story of why they cannot complete this task and if you were truly a team player, you would take care of it.

The best way to handle all these folks is gently but firmly. Give them the things you love about them and then gently advise them of some changes they must make in for you to focus and succeed.

Day 7- Health. Today we will look at your mental health and ask questions about what thoughts are most common in your mind? You need to inventory your negative thoughts. In your notebook, write down the common negative thoughts that you are fully aware of right now. An example would be, constantly stating, "I can't, I shouldn't, and wouldn't it have been great if I had done this instead."

These types of statements that many people say to themselves, grind into the brain, and cause depression and anxiety. You become unable to put your total focus in a partnership or a task at work, because you are currently unable to stay on track and drift into the, "wow, this is hard, I can't do it."

When that starts to happen, it can snowball and become an avalanche of remembering times that you were unable to do something and just gave up.

You need to change the statements.

For example, "I can't," becomes "this is giving me some grief right now, but I am going to slam dunk it in the end."

When your mental game is not on point, you can not only suffer from the "I cannot," to having a serious bout of depression. If you are feeling blue frequently, make a list of what you feel may be causing it. Are you eating properly, exercising, talking out your frustrations with family or friends? These are your first go-to things to do when you are blue.

Of course, it never hurts to see your doctor and get some advice. Explain how you feel and how it hurts your ability to focus on the truly important things in life.

Day 8-Physical health. Without good physical health, it is difficult to focus. What areas can you improve on?

Make a list of your current exercise items and the amount of time per day that you spend on it. People like Dwayne "The Rock" Johnson have superior focus and goal achieving abilities because of their physical health. Dwayne starts his serious workout routine at 4:30 am.

Now make notes beside your list of how you can improve. If you wrote down that you ride your bike for 30 minutes a day, ask yourself how much did your heart rate increase? Did you sweat? Are your muscles tired…a good tired that will promote a healthy sleep?

When you note that perhaps you are just easy riding, strive to change it. Pick a different route with some hills. Or change your speed. Go slow, sprint, slow down, and sprint again.

Do a complete survey of your physical regime now.

Day 9-What are you fueling your body with? Want laser focus? Eat the right food today.

List out your breakfast, lunch, and supper and include the snacks. Include the beverages. You want mostly water and some freshly squeezed citrus or vegetable juice in there.

Okay, examples of what should be in each list.

For breakfast, we should see something like blueberries or avocados. For lunch or supper, some fish that is high in fat. Sardines make a great lunch and fresh mackerel with pineapple is delicious while being awesome for focus.

The snacks need to be nuts or seeds high in omega 3, not potato chips. If these items and more are not on your list, then cross out the bad stuff and add in all the good food we just mentioned. Get fueling for focus today.

Day 10-What do you focus on in your business? The so-called, failures or learning to improve from mistakes? Rarely does one have a job outside the home or as a freelancer, that days go by before you make a serious blunder. One of the reasons why people make these mistakes in business is their lack of focus.

When you rush through a job, you miss items that might be listed in a contract or write an important sales email and forget to mention a detail that is highly important to get your customers signature.

Dwelling on the mistakes is not the answer. Focus is your correct path.

In your notebook, write out what you consider are mistakes you have made in business over the last month. Next to that, write, "I forgive myself." You need to accept that it happened, forgive yourself for your errors, and focus on creating fewer mistakes. It will never be perfect.

Now write down, why these mistakes happened? Ask yourself if you rushed, had too many distractions or didn't fully understand what was required? In a high-tech world, if you are not focusing on knowing everything you can about your subject, then you are putting yourself at disadvantage.

Finally write down what you are going to do, to focus and improve.

Day 11-Finance. Are you very loose with your money, have zero focus on what you spend every day and what money comes into your account every day? You need to chart your money. You may not be aware that you are overspending on coffee, outside lunches; gas when you could have taken a bus for example.

You also need to chart what you bring in each day. This is especially true if you are a freelancer. Know your budget and look where to cut.

Your action for today is to come up with a way to chart your finances. Use an excel spreadsheet or something else.

As well, you need to sit down in a quiet space and go over all your bills. Quite frankly, if you are not doing this, you are likely being overcharged for services. You want to be debt free, right? Of course you do. Start your plan to be debt free today. In your notebook, look at where you can free money up and put it on your mortgage for starters. Ask yourself hard questions.

Ask if you need to have all those cable services, that add up to $150 or more a month. You get the picture and you can do this.

Focusing on your finances will free you from money anxiety and depression.

Day 12-Build wealth. Having money will allow you the freedom and ability to give. It has been shown that when you give, the universe gives back to you in abundance. Start with the basics and work your way up.

Your action plan today is to go to the library. Check out "The Wealthy Barber," by Dave Chilton. This is an excellent book that will get you started. Why are you not buying this book? Well, the answer is simple. You are going to focus on tracking your money, being debt-free, and building wealth from this day forward. Don't pay for this book. The cost to buy in a book store is just plain outrageous and yes you can get it on Kindle but why even lay out a dime if you don't have to.

Grab this book today and take serious notes, then put an action plan together on how to focus on all matters related to your money.

Day 13-Growth. In building focus, learn to grow in your knowledge. Feeding the computer between your ears gives you a wealth of knowledge and the ability to focus on what is important...focus, self-confidence and self-esteem plus, for many people, spirituality.

Your action plan today is…stop looking at memes while on the toilet. Sort of a joke, but maybe not, depending on how long you hang out there.

To be serious though, you have downtime that could be used to build your focus, self-confidence, and grow in the other areas mentioned.

Today, you will start with these podcasts and then search for others that fill your needs.

https://www.theminimalists.com/p036/

https://player.fm/series/courageous-self-confidence

Day 14-How many books did you read last year? How many documentaries did you watch?

When you watch mindless television, it numbs your brain. The dumbing down of society has been attributed by some…to the proliferation of game shows and reality shows. Feed your mind, like you would a healthy body and it will respond and make your life successful.

Your action plan today is to drop the garbage television and seek out documentaries that will enrich your life.

Next, you will make a list of books related to focus. Since many people do not like to read, that doesn't let them off the hook from doing this action plan.

Non-readers will search the library system for talking books on focus.

To get you started…search your library for "The 7 Laws of Focus."

Day 15-Meetups. There are meetups for everything under the sun. Meetups are a great way to get out of the house and socialize while learning new things.

Get googling today and find a meetup for focus in your city. If there are none, then start one. That's right, you can take the leadership role and start your very own meetup group. Then invite people you know who are already great at having laser focus and invite them to share their knowledge.

People love to teach what they know, and this is an opportunity that can reap other rewards. You can gently network with people in your meetup group. Perhaps you are looking for a new career and this may put you in touch with someone who has connections in your chosen field.

Day 16-Personal projects. Your career is going great. You have a fabulous relationship with your partner and the best friends in the world. Life couldn't be better. Your health is awesome and yet something is missing.

Think about your life and what you do for others. Are you a giver? Chances are, that you invest more in others than you do yourself.

When you focus so intently on others but not so much on yourself, you can burn out. It is very important to love yourself and put some serious focus on who you are and what you bring to this world.

In your notebook, write down what you do for yourself. After a few minutes, if your page is blank, then visualize what you would like to do for yourself.

Would you like to paint or write a story? If you feel that you lack artistic talent, then what else could you do?

Write down the idea of hiking in a spot where not many people go. Think about going there just by yourself and bring one of those comfortable hiking chairs. Make a note where you can buy one. Write down what you would do. Would you sit and breathe the fresh air?

Would you focus on wildlife, like the birds and the squirrels, or use the time to do some meditation?

You need to invest in your well-being on focus on creating the best you. Decide and take action today on YOU.

Day 17-Plan for focus. Okay, we are getting close to the end of our focus challenge. The next few things we are going to put into action, all go together and will make your ability to focus and succeed rock.

For a couple of these items, you will need to spend a small amount, but it will be worth it and pay you back in spades.

You need to plan your focus. A good focus planner takes all the elements of focus, goal setting, and steps to action-binding them together to make a very strong program for yourself.

Today look for a focus planner and start working on it. If you need to save time or aren't sure what to get or where…then have a look at the link below:

https://fullfocusplanner.com/?v

Day 18-Journal. To go hand in hand with your focus planner, use a focus journal. The journal linked below is specifically designed to help you journal about productivity and goals. It is specially created so that it lays flat for easy writing. The interior design is based on bullet journaling.

Get your journal today and start working on building that laser focus.

https://www.thefocusjournal.co/products/the-focus-journal

Day 19-Visualizing. You took action and got your planner and your journal for focus. Now perhaps you are stuck on what to put in these items.

This is the perfect time to practice visualizing.

The best 3-point shooters in basketball are experts who are visualizing. In their minds eye, they repeatedly see the ball arcing through the air and swooshing through the net without touching the rim.

To achieve focus and clarity, you need to practice visualizing in your mind, what you want from life. See it in full detail and add sounds that enhance the feeling of success.

Your challenge today, is to practice visualizing off and on throughout the day. It takes practice to slow your mind and then see the big beautiful picture. Set aside quiet time and visualize as much as your day will allow. Then practice a short visualization each time before you write.

Take today to create a vision board. These are also sometimes called focus boards, especially if they are used in a team atmosphere in business. In this case, all the items on the board would have to appeal to everyone, so a lot of thought goes into the creation.

To do your focus board, decide what your number one focus is at this very minute. Is it to lose weight and enjoy the process? Or have you been stuck in an apartment for far too long and with X number of children?

Today you will create a focus board the simple way. Go to the store and get one piece of plain poster board, the kind that kids use in school projects all the time. If you don't already have colored markers or pencils, get some of those too.

Your vision board is going to be placed above the desk you use to write in your planner/journal.

Your fun task is to find pictures that relate to the type of house you want to focus on buying if that is your vision for today. You'll need some free real estate magazines and maybe some paid magazines on houses. If you have a good quality printer, then you can find images for you to download, cut out, and focus on.

Put your board together with all the images you get and with your colored pencils, doodle in things that will motivate you to focus on these goals. You don't have to write in straight lines, so if you are doing a collage type of board, go right ahead and slant, "I will buy this house in one year's time," alongside the house that gets your juices flowing the most.

Day 20-Subliminal works wonders for many people. Subliminal messages enter your brain, bypassing the subconscious mind's steel doors. The positive messages remove the negative thoughts that have dominated your thinking for years.

You can use focus subliminal video to back up what you have been doing to build focus or go deep if you are having trouble being focused.

Your action today is to give this subliminal a listen. Then decide if this is something you want to incorporate into your daily focus routine.

https://youtu.be/-ZDQB6dbCq8

Remember that if at first, you don't have success, don't give up. Search for a different subliminal video. Not all creators are equal.

Day 21-Apps are your final challenge. The use of apps in goal setting and time management is very important.

To finally put this challenge altogether, we are going to look at focus apps. There are a number of them out there but for your final challenge, we will get you to look at the app below today:

https://www.focusboosterapp.com/

This app not only gets you super focused, but it is based on a time management idea called the Pomodoro technique. This technique has you focusing on one task for 25 minutes, followed by a short break and then another 25 minutes of work. Check it out today and use it right away.

We are at the end of your 21-day Focus Challenge. You should be miles ahead of where you were before you started this challenge. Here is the best thing for you to do. Do not just stop dead in your tracks. Go back and review your challenge as many times as you need. Make adjustments that help you focus better. Always remember the story of planes and boats. They start a point **A** focused on getting to point **B** safely. Along the way, they get battered by high winds and waves pushing them off course. They need to focus and alter their course when necessary to get back on track.

You have the tools now and here is to your success.

Bonus 3

75+ Ways to Take Action, Stay Focused and Get Motivated

TIPS FOR TAKING ACTION

Tip Number 1: Just do it.

The first step is always the hardest. Your mind will come up with all sorts of scenarios to prevent you from taking that scary first step toward your goal. That does not mean you are a coward, though. It is just your brain's way of defending yourself.

Sometimes, though, you must listen to what your heart has to say and *just do it*. Everything else will be a lot easier once you get past the first hurdle – and that is to ignore your brain's dire warnings and go with your gut instinct.

Tip Number 2: Doing something is not always a *physical* thing.

It is understandable if you mistook the need for taking action as doing something literally or physically. Yet you see, there are many other ways for you to take action without even lifting a finger. For that matter, consider the act of *planning*.

It is never wise to try achieving a goal without a plan. If you want to spend the least amount of time and effort in achieving your goal, then you need to come up with a step-by-step plan for accomplishing it.

A good plan considers all potential consequences as well as all the possible avenues you may take in order to reach your objective.

Tip Number 3: Breathing helps.

Are you feeling nervous or nauseous? It is normal to feel uneasy about doing anything to reach your goal. Acting is often synonymous to taking risk. You are nervous because you know that risks can either end with success or failure, and who wants to end up failing?

Whenever you feel like there is a panic attack coming in, just take a deep breath. Better yet, take several deep breaths. Studies show how breathing can effectively clear the mind and help calm your nerves. So, go ahead and breathe - inhale all the way from your stomach to take full advantage!

Tip Number 4: Take a page from the most successful books.

You may think that you are the only one suffering a certain kind of problem of a certain magnitude in this world, but you are not. With a little research, you are sure to find something in common with ordinary and extraordinary people.

You may not be a U.S. President like Bill Clinton, but you are running for a position and you have limited funds like Clinton for your campaign. What did Clinton do that you can do as well? In the end, it is all about finding the small but essential similarities.

Tip Number 5: Take baby steps.

Do not push yourself to achieve the same things with the same amount of time and resources the way other people had done. In the end, you have to remind yourself that every person is unique and, consequently, his own set of strengths and weaknesses.

Also, it could be that you are just starting out and the other person you are comparing yourself to is years ahead of you in terms of expertise and experience. The other person *cannot* afford to take baby steps, but you can, and you should!

If you rush things too much, everything may end up backfiring on you.

Tip Number 6: Rome was not built in a day.

This is obviously related to the above tip, but it is different in the way that it considers what you want to do with your time.

It is good to have a plan for everything, but you do not have to accomplish everything in a single day. Even if you have the energy to do so, the people around you and who also have something at stake in reaching your shared goals may not have the time and similar energy to do so.

Give them a break. If all of you have truly worked hard, then all you deserve to rest. There is always tomorrow to think about.

Tip Number 7: Do not pressure yourself.

Pressuring yourself is different from motivating yourself. Motivating yourself will get you to take action while pressuring yourself will only succeed in freezing your limbs and brain cells into a state of inaction.

There are sure to be other people and other sources you will receive a lot of flak and pressure about getting things done. Why burden yourself with more pressure when you can give yourself a pep talk instead?

Tip Number 8: A little competition is good – just do not make a big deal out of it.

Competition can make you take action because the more you delay, the further behind you will be in achieving your goal. Friendly competition is also effective for staying focused and getting you pumped up but be careful!

If you let yourself focus too much on the competition, then you may end up forgetting about the bigger picture. In the end, being too competitive may be another source of distraction that you absolutely do not need.

Tip Number 9: Believe in yourself.

Taking action requires you to have faith in yourself – especially when everyone around you is telling you that you cannot do it. In the end, you have to remember that you know yourself best. You know what you are capable of, and if you believe that the goal you have in mind is well within your reach, then it truly is – no matter what others may say.

Tip Number 10: Get a companion.

Just because you have someone with you and willing to help you out does not mean you were not strong enough to accomplish your goal. It also does not make your goal any less satisfying. If anything, the goal becomes sweeter because you have someone to share it with!

If you feel that you need your wife to be at your side to accomplish a particular goal, then go and make it happen and again – forget about what anyone else has to say. As long as you are not hurting yourself or anyone else, then there is nothing wrong with what you are doing.

Tip Number 11: Get someone to do it for you.

Taking action also does not mean that you have to do everything alone. Say your goal is to build a house. Does that mean you should do everything, from putting up boards and painting the walls? Of course not!

Taking action may also mean finding the best person to do the job. So, do not be shy to admit if something is well beyond your actual KSAs (knowledge, skills, and abilities). There are just some things in life that are better left in the hands of an expert.

Tip Number 12: Do not be too proud to ask for help.

A lot of people confuse taking action as doing something that directly contributes to achieving a particular goal. What they fail to understand is that sometimes, indirect benefits also matter just as much.

Consider, for instance, the act of forgetting about your pride. Some people may say that it has nothing to do with achieving a certain type of goal, but

what if it is your pride that is holding you back from getting much-needed help from an expert?

Tip Number 13: It is okay to start again.

What if there comes a point in time that you realize that the first step you took was actually the wrong one? Or what if you suddenly realize that what you are doing is not taking you toward your goal but away from it?

Do you just sit down and cry over spilt milk? If so, that is not equivalent to taking action. You may be doing something, but it is nothing that can help you achieve your goal.

If you realize that something is wrong, then clear your mind and retrace your steps until you find out that critical mistake you committed. Correct it and move on. If you have to, start from scratch – the sooner, the better!

Tip Number 14: Never stop trying!

As mentioned earlier on, the process of achieving one's goal is never ending. Taking action also means that you have to get back to your feet if you stumble or fall. It is even okay if you have to start all over again. In the end, what is critical is that you do not let your failures keep you from continuously taking action and moving forward.

So, go ahead and pick yourself up, dust yourself off, and learn from your mistakes. You will be a better and stronger person for doing this!

Tip Number 15: Have a back-up plan.

Plans – just like rules – are meant to be broken. And you need to be prepared for that eventuality right from the start by having a contingency or back-up plan ready.

Others feel that back-up plans are akin to admitting failure. It is not. Rather, back-up plans are actually a mere way of acknowledging the fact that change is the only thing that is constant in the world. There is no way for you to predict what is going to happen in the next minute, but you *can* try to prepare for things that could happen.

Think of it as smoothing the way to taking action toward achieving your goal.

Tip Number 16: Consider your resources.

Taking action gives you direction but that is not what it is all about. You also have to consider the resources you have on hand. How do you make the most out of it? What other resources do you need in order to make a move? Where can you get it?

Willpower and motivation as well as focus are all great things to have but these are *internal* resources. You also have to back up your plan with external and concrete resources like money, manpower, and skills.

Tip Number 17: Look before you leap but leap all the same if you have to!

There are two kinds of risks: manageable and unmanageable. You are lucky if all the things you have to do to reach your goal involve manageable risks. But what if it is not? Should you back out instead and let all your previous hard work go to waste?

Risks are scary, and it is a good thing that you are aware of that. Those who think that they can take on any kind of risk are simply foolhardy and reckless. They are certainly not brave or exceptionally smart.

If you come across an unmanageable risk or one where the stakes are too high, do look before you leap. Consider the ups and downs, but most importantly of all – consider what your brain and guts have to say. Then leap – and leap high – if you really need to!

Tip Number 18: Do not be too rigid or stubborn.

You have to know when to give up and change tactics. On paper, your plan may look fool proof and absolutely brilliant but a lot of things in the real world are unpredictable and can mess up with your plan.

You have to know when to stop knocking yourself against the wall and find another way toward reaching your goal. Remember: when there is a will, there is a way. If your Plan A did not work, what else is your Plan B good for if you are not willing to use it?

Tip Number 19: Do not wait for things to happen. Make it happen instead!

The most successful people in live are always those who are active participants in life rather. Instead of passively waiting, hoping, and wishing that something would happen to them – people who are go-getters do not hesitate to act proactively and make things happen.

They are not the kind to wait for a sign from the fates or a falling star to appear in the sky before they get moving. If they have a goal in sight, and they have a plan for achieving it, then they will move heaven and earth to get it.

Tip Number 20: Give yourself a reasonable deadline.

Existing commitments may be a valid reason for preventing you from taking action completely to achieving your goal, but you also have to understand that these commitments are never going to go away. They are there for life. It is therefore unreasonable to keep pushing off the need to take a proactive stand because of your "commitments".

You have to be firm with yourself and give yourself a deadline. Sometimes, that is the only way to get things done.

Tip Number 21: Be decisive.

When you do commit yourself to a plan and take action, do be decisive about it. This will help smooth things up more and make it easier for you to achieve your goal. If you are in a leadership position, people are unlikely to have faith in your decision if they can see that you yourself do not have faith in what you are doing.

You have to show them that you know what needs to be done and you have the power to help everyone reach their goals – if they follow you.

TIPS FOR STAYING FOCUSED!

Tip Number 22: Make a checklist.

Checklists show you where you are, how much you have progressed, and what still needs to be done in order to achieve your goal.

Even if you suddenly fall sick and have to leave the office for a week, the moment you get back your all-important checklist will be enough to bring you up to speed.

Tip Number 23: Set a schedule.

The quickest way to reaching your goal is to create a schedule for it – and stick to it. How many hours each day can you truly set aside for reaching your goal? What part of the day is the best time to work on reaching your goal?

A schedule also means having a specific place for you to do your work. Choose something that will benefit the kind of work that you are doing and the kind of person you are. Will something peaceful and quiet work more for you or do you prefer to be working outdoors and surrounded by sounds of nature?

Tip Number 23: Make it a habit.

It is not enough, of course, to simply make a schedule. After all, creating one is easy – it is the "doing" part that is difficult. To make it easier for you to keep to your schedule, you have to turn it into a habit. Treat it as an integral part of your day that you absolutely cannot miss.

Your body does not automatically search for caffeine in the morning just because it wants to. It was trained to do so by repetitive action, strengthened by your own desire for a delicious cup of coffee. Your mind also does not look for its daily fix of quiz shows in the evenings for no reason. It was trained to do so as well.

So why can't you train yourself to make your goal achievement schedule a part of your daily routine as well?

Tip Number 24: No excuses!

It is critical that you do not allow yourself any excuses. If you do, then the excuses will never stop. Your body has a "giving-in" muscle and every time you give in, it gets more powerful. Before you know it, that muscle has been flexed so much that it is impossible to ignore.

Tip Number 25: If you really have to, then it is okay to negotiate the terms – but do keep your word.

There are times when no matter how hard you try; you just cannot find the energy to do the work. Or perhaps you are too occupied or excited by something else that your focus on achieving your goal is absolutely ruined.

At times like this, there really is no other option left but to "negotiate" the terms of your schedule. If you are supposed to work four hours today yet you can only work three, then work an extra hour tomorrow or the day after.

It is important to specify the date for your negotiated term and of course to keep your word to yourself. This, however, is one thing that you absolutely must not make a habit of!

Tip Number 26: Eliminate distraction.

Distraction is your focus' greatest enemy. Like temptation, it is insidious and will find all sorts of ways to mess with your concentration. Before you even start working, you should start by eliminating all possible sources of distraction.

Distraction can also be internal. These are those niggling doubts and worries that do nothing to help you reach your goal. You need to practice pushing them to the back of your mind. Keep practicing and they soon will not be a bother at all!

Tip Number 27: Log out from all social networking and social messaging systems as well as Internet forums.

You may say that you find lots of great information and are able to stay connected with your network or market by keeping yourself online, but surely your personal life or business can exist for a few hours without being on the Twitter and Facebook radar?

No matter how you look at it, in the end, Twitter, Facebook, forums and all other ways to communicate with people online will only be a potential source of distraction.

If you must, set a separate schedule for it – but this is one activity that should not be a part of your multitasking list.

Tip Number 28: Meditate.

Numerous studies have already proven that meditation techniques – just like breathing exercises – are helpful in clearing your mind *and* improving your focus. If the words and figures that you are supposed to analyse are blurring right before your eyes, it is the time to meditate. If your anger or resentment is making it difficult for you to concentrate, meditating will also do the trick.

You do not need to chant any mantras to meditate – although if you feel it will help, go ahead and do so. But in any case, finding a quiet place to sit and close your eyes and let your mind wander freely is good enough.

Do try *not* to lie down while meditating as you may end up sleeping instead.

Tip Number 29: Take a time-out but time it!

Sometimes, you can get a little burned out if you have been working too hard for the past few days. When this happens, it is okay to take a little breather from your work schedule.

Of course, time-outs cannot last forever so do make sure that you time it as well. If you are working only for a few hours, then fifteen to thirty minutes should be enough. If, however, your schedule encompasses the whole day, then an hour at the most would be sufficient. Anything longer than that may make you too lazy enough to get back to work.

Tip Number 30: Are You Sleeping Enough?

This is one of those cases when science has the last say, and according to its experts, sleep can have a significant impact on your ability to concentrate. Having enough hours of sleep will improve your concentration. Having too little or too much of it, however, would cause you problems with staying focused.

To get enough sleep every night, you should try keeping regular hours or at least have a fixed schedule for sleeping. Eliminate all sources of distraction as well. Consider this as another goal for you to focus on and take action for.

Tip Number 31: Diet matters.

Diet also has to do with your ability to stay focused. A proper and healthy meal plan for the day will go a long way in improving your mind's ability to work and increase your stamina. Make sure you also take in enough vitamins and minerals as well. If necessary, take health supplements.

Tip Number 32: Exercise matters as well.

Again, you may argue that exercising may not have anything to do with helping you save money for your first car or reaching this month's sales quota, but it does.

Or at least that is what most scientific studies are suggesting. Like meditating, sleeping, and the right, a sufficient amount of daily exercise will also help improve the state of your mind. That you will get fitter and look more fabulous are just icing on the cake!

Tip Number 33: Enjoy what you are doing.

Find a way to make the process of achieving your goal enjoyable. Sometimes, it only takes a change of scenery. Other times, you just have to find the right angle to look at your situation.

When you are doing something you love, such as baking, reading, or dancing, then you absolutely have no problems concentrating, don't you? But if you are being forced to do something you hate, then only with the greatest effort are you able to keep yourself focused on your work.

Tip Number 34: How about a change of pace?

Focus is also dependent on pace. You may be trying to do things too fast or slow for your brain to actually *enjoy* what you are doing.

When your pace is too punishingly fast, you are more liable to commit mistakes. In your effort to save yourself time, you are actually causing yourself to suffer greater delays since some of your tasks have to be redone or rectified.

Using an excessively slow or relaxing pace is no good either. Do not overestimate your ability to work because that can ultimately develop into procrastination if you are not careful.

Tip Number 35: Consider a change of setting.

Sometimes, working in the same place day in and day out can get a little boring, and your mind will start to wander – relentlessly. When you have tried your best to keep your mind from wandering to no avail, then a change of setting may be in order.

Look for a different place – just for a day or two – to stay when it is time to work on achieving your goal. A new place may be enough to spark your interest in your goals. It may also help get your creative juices flowing and give you an idea or two on how to better motivate yourself.

Tip Number 36: Be methodical.

The best way to stay focused is to be methodical. Do not choose a random point to start working toward your goal. Whatever it is you are aiming for — even if it is to improve your marriage or lose weight — there is sure to be a methodical or logical system for doing it.

Taking a methodical approach helps improve your focus because it enables you to see where you are going. If you are feeling a little bored concentrating on the task at hand, you can switch your attention to making the necessary adjustments to prepare for the tasks in line.

Tip Number 37: Music is --- fifty/fifty.

The truth is some people find music relaxing and helpful to their work. Others, however, find it too relaxing that they end up sleeping or they find it too entertaining that they end up forgetting all about the task at hand.

You have to determine for yourself if music will serve as an aid to improving your focus or a distraction instead?

Tip Number 38: It is all about what you think and feel.

Well-meaning friends may encourage you to try this and that to improve focus. Certainly, there is nothing wrong with taking their words into account. Remember, however, that every person is built differently. What may work for them may not work for you. That does not mean, however, only one of you is doing the right thing.

In the end, the best way to improve your focus is to do what works for *you* and not others.

Tip Number 39: Do not be a pushover.

Some people will try to sway your mind and make you feel guilty about the time you are devoting to your goal. Whatever it may be, if your goal is important to you and is not cruel or harmful to yourself or anyone, then you have all the right in the world to devote yourself to it.

Tip Number 40: Do not allow emotional conflicts to get in your way.

One of the worst kinds of distraction is emotional conflict. This kind of problem eats away at your concentration. If there is anything that is bothering you, resolve it right away before getting back to work.

Do not allow it to fester inside you. The longer you delay resolving such conflicts, the harder a time you will have finding a way to re-open the discussion about it.

Tip Number 41: Know your priorities.

If you are torn between doing two things, you have to give yourself another ultimatum. Which is the more important priority – the goal you are working on or the alternative?

Be brutally frank to yourself as you consider your options. If you have to choose which of the two you should lose, which of them are you willing to give up?

Tip Number 42: Consider your energy patterns.

This may sound a little too scientific, but rest assured that it is not. People have different energy patterns for various reasons. Some people, for instance, simply feel more energized to work in the middle of the night because there is absolutely no distraction to worry about, with everyone fast asleep.

Others like to work first thing in the morning because it makes them feel productive. Their energy then wanes when it gets to lunch time but jumps back up when it is in the early evening.

Try to familiarize yourself with your energy pattern. Think back on the days you were asked to complete a particular task. When are you typically more efficient in completing your work? When are you less than diligent working on your tasks?

Tip Number 43: Maximize your time.

Maximize your time in the sense that you should delegate what may be delegated to other capable individuals, thus allowing you to concentrate on the most critical tasks.

Your focus will be ruined if you have a million things to do and yet you are worrying the most about only three of them. If this is the case, you will never get to finish *anything*.

Do yourself a favor. Find people whom you can trust to do a part of your work and then devote yourself to doing what you feel needs the most of your attention.

Tip Number 44: Chew things down into manageable pieces.

Say you were given one whole cake to eat. Should you swallow it down in one bite? It would be pretty impossible to make an entire cake fit your mouth, but you can definitely eat it all if you cut it into several slices. From there, you can eat a slice of cake one bite after another.

Sometimes, focusing on the bigger picture alone is not helpful. There are times when you have to forget about the bigger picture first and concentrate on one part of the picture at a time.

Tip Number 45: Make allowances for mistakes.

Nobody is perfect. There will be times when nothing you can do is right. It is critical that you prepare beforehand for this and make allowances for mistakes.

If you can complete a task for thirty minutes, try giving yourself forty minutes instead. This way, you will not be terribly backed up if you do end up making a mistake or two. Giving yourself allowances will also prevent your mistakes from breaking your stride. You will keep going – no matter what – like an Energizer bunny!

Tip Number 46: Practice memory improvement techniques.

Memory and focus are intertwined in many ways. As such, improving your memory will consequently improve your ability to concentrate.

There are many ways to improve your concentration. You can find free exercises online. You can also try joining a memory training workshop or read a memory enhancement book. There are also memory training software programs that you could try.

Tip Number 47: Learn how to read effectively.

Whether your goal is personal, work-related or something else, there will surely be a time when your goal would require you to read something. This should not be a problem, however, if you learn how to read effectively.

The world's fastest readers do not really read every word of the book or material they are reading. Rather, most speed readers are good at skimming and finding context clues. Their mind and eyes are trained to find the most important parts of each page and paragraph. Even if they have a limited amount of time to finish reading something, they will not have any problems grasping the most salient points about it.

The written word is one of the most notoriously common things that many people have a hard time focusing on. You will not have to su3ffer the same fate if you just take the time to learn how to read effectively.

Tip Number 48: Be eager to learn.

No one is too smart to stop learning. You will have an easier time focusing on new topics or tasks if train yourself *not* to be reluctant to learn about new things.

Granted, old dogs have a hard time learning new tricks, but surely you have more brain cells and willpower than canines?

Knowledge is a beautiful thing, and you should not turn your back on the opportunity to learn something new if it is given to you.

Tip Number 49: If you are the type and if it helps – *pray*.

Religion is purely personal – just like goals are. If prayer matters to a lot to you, then asking for a little bit of divine intervention would not go amiss. As the Bible says, *ask and ye shall receive.*

Other religions in the world are surely of the same mind even if they couch it in different terms.

Tip Number 50: Remind yourself of the consequences.

If you are extremely tempted to give up on what you are doing and just lose yourself in having fun instead, remind yourself of the possible consequences and that is sure to get you back in line.

Say you want to lose weight. If you eat that extra cup of rice tonight, it will mean having to spend an extra hour in the gym tomorrow. If you fail to do that, it will mean having your weight increase by two pounds. In time, it will mean not being able to fit into that new swimsuit you so wanted to wear to the beach party you are planning to attend – which the guy of your dreams is sure to attend as well.

Now ask yourself again – do you still want to stray from the task at hand?

Tip Number 51: Remind yourself that you are not the only one at stake.

Most of the time, the goals you want to achieve affect others as well. Say it is your aim to increase profits by 25% by the end of the year. If you do not reach your goal in time, then you will not be able to give your staff the Christmas party and end-of-the-year bonuses they so richly deserve.

If you do not care about the consequences you will suffer from by losing focus, surely you are not *selfish* enough to ignore how your decision will impact others?

Tip Number 52: Forward all calls to your voice mail box.

Phones – all types of it – are also a source of distraction. Change your answering machine's message to let people know that you absolutely cannot afford to be disturbed. If they genuinely care about you, they are sure to understand.

Be sure, however, to let them know that you will be checking your email inbox every hour. If they have a drastic need to contact you, then they better start typing their emails.

Tip Number 53: Limit you email-checking to five minutes per hour.

It really cannot be more than that because you are only supposed to reply to emails that are absolutely require a response. Anything less than important should be set aside. You have to be very firm about this rule or you will end up procrastinating again.

TIPS TO GET MOTIVATED!

Tip Number 54: Remember that checklist? Do not forget to tick it off!

Seeing your checklist near to completion will always work as a great boost to your confidence. If you were able to accomplish so much already, surely you can accomplish the rest of your tasks?

Tip Number 55: Use affirmations.

Affirmations are basically positive statements that you tell to yourself repeatedly like a mantra. These are supposed to help you enjoy a positive frame of mind and be more confident about accomplishing your goal.

Some people say that affirmations should not use potential forms of verbs like "I can". In order to further convince themselves of their abilities, affirmations should start with words such as "I will…" and "I am…" because you are *that* sure about yourself.

Tip Number 56: Think of *internal* rewards to congratulate yourself.

Positive reinforcement is always a good thing so do not forget to give yourself a pat on the back when you have completed one of the most fundamental steps to achieving your goal.

Now is the time to start tweeting about your latest task. Let yourself bask in the praise of your loved ones and friends as this will surely get you going.

Tip Number 57: Reward yourself materially as well.

Material rewards certainly matter, too. It does not have anything extravagant although if it is something you can afford and genuinely want, then you can also promise yourself a big reward when you reach your goal.

Try to be a little creative about your rewards. You can pamper yourself with a massage, take a trip out of town, or allow yourself a night out dining in the most expensive restaurant in the area.

It can also be something as simple as letting yourself laze the weekend away doing nothing and enjoying other small luxuries that you usually do not have time for.

Ultimately, just think about what will make you happy – and do it!

Tip Number 58: Reassess your goal.

Sometimes, the reason why you have a hard time motivating yourself is because your goal is no longer important. From time to time, you should re-evaluate your goal and find out if it still as important or it needs a little redefining.

Tip Number 59: Always search for the brighter side.

Do not think that there is *no* brighter side because there always is. If you feel you have hit rock bottom, there is still a bright side. When you are down, there is no way else but *up!*

Tip Number 60: Look for a role model.

A role model does not have to be someone perfect, famous, or even older than you. Rather, that role model has qualities that you so admire, and you wish to have because you will become a better person for it.

When you feel like giving up, think about your role model. No one is immune to having temptations, but every person has the power to say 'no' to it. Your role model was strong enough to say 'no' to distraction and stay focused. Surely you can do it, too?

In the end, both of you are flesh and blood mortals – capable of doing the same thing as long as you put your mind to it.

Tip Number 61: Search for inspiration.

Role models are different from inspiration. Role models are someone you try to emulate. People, things, or places to inspire you are also like goals, though. Why is becoming wealthy your goal? It is because you want to give your parents a chance to retire early. Then your parents are your inspiration.

When you are extremely frustrated about what is happening and you feel like throwing the towel, picture your parents and what they will be like if they have to continue working for years in spite of their frail health.

Tip Number 62: Do not fail to take advantage of the power of visualization.

It is easier to keep yourself motivated when you are able to visualize reaching your dream. Close your eyes and try to imagine what would happen if you were to reach your goal. How would it feel? What would happen afterwards?

Make it so vivid that you can actually feel the joy of reaching your dream.

Tip Number 63: Proverbs are there for a reason.

If you have noticed, proverbs and old sayings have been used throughout the book quite frequently. That is because they are true. Clichés have become clichés because they have been said too often and are essentially facts.

If there are no words you can think of personally to get yourself motivated, do not hesitate to call in the power of proverbs.

Tip Number 64: Talk to children.

Kids say the darnedest things indeed, but they also often have an ingenuous way of seeing things. With their views untainted by cynicism and greed, children can get you back to seeing the world with rose-colored glasses.

Tip Number 65: *Carpe diem!*

That is Latin for 'seize the day' if you have forgotten. Tell yourself that the opportunity your goal represents comes only once in a lifetime. If you do not seize the day – or the moment for that matter – then that chance may never come again.

Are you willing to take that risk?

Tip Number 66: Think of the last time you worked against all odds – and won.

You are a powerful person yet sometimes you may need to remind yourself of it. If your confidence has taken a nosedive for any reason, think back of the last time that you worked against all odds. Think of the time that no one had your back and only you had faith in yourself. Think of the time you had taken the role of an underdog – and won.

You did it then. You can do it again. Just believe!

Tip Number 67: Join motivation seminars now and then.

If you have never tried attending a motivation seminar, it is easy for you to say that these so-called self-help gurus are just out to con you out of your money. But why not give it a try? At the most, you will only lose a couple of dollars for attending. Yet what if it works? Then you would have gained so much more!

If you have no idea which of today's many inspirational speakers is the best, do not hesitate to ask for recommendations. Check the Internet for reviews as well.

Tip Number 68: Remember the little things.

Motivation is also a matter of point of view. If you are tired of working or doing something for the sake of achieving your goal alone, then do it just for the sake of it.

Do it because you are having fun doing it. Do it because you love it and it makes you feel good. Sometimes, the journey counts more than the actual destination.

Tip Number 69: Keep a gratitude journal.

If Oprah herself does this, then surely everyone has the propensity to benefit from it as well? For each day, try to think of as many things as you can that you are sincerely thankful for.

If you feel that you have absolutely nothing to be thankful about, then you are wrong. You are alive, aren't you? You can still read this and perhaps take up a pen and write your first post in your thank you journal, can't you? Then that already gives you three reasons to be thankful about.

Remember: motivation is a matter of perspective. If you cannot see it from one angle, then you probably could in another.

Tip Number 70: Are you tempted to give up? Do (Insert Number Here) more.

When you feel like you have reached the end of your tether, make one last big push by doing 5 more. Or if you are just one step away from giving in to exhaustion or sleep then do just 3 or even just one more!

You may not have completed your schedule for today but knowing that you gave it your best is enough to give you an energetic and motivated for the next day.

Tip Number 71: Failure is *not* an option.

Granted, you are not stuck in the moon, flying in Apollo 11, but does it really matter? You just have to imagine yourself in the same back-against-the-wall scenario and that is sure to be motivation enough to work hard.

Earlier, you have learned how it is to get past failure and the importance of *not* beating yourself up about it. Even so, that does not mean you can get away with never worrying about it.

Tip Number 72: Never say never – unless it is to say you will *never* quit.

You may change tactics, rest for a while, and redefine your goal but none of those means you are quitting. Never should *never* be a part of your vocabulary – even if that sounds contradictory; the moment you start entertaining doubts is the moment you start losing.

Tip Number 73: Aim to be *better* and not perfect.

Aiming to be perfect is like aiming for the moon. You will never be able to reach for it with your hands. But what you can do is to improve yourself and make yourself or your situation better.

You may not be able to reach for the moon, but if you were to arm yourself with a telescope, then the moon could get closer to you instead.

Tip Number 74: Hope for the best but prepare for the worst.

Motivation can be a double-edged sword. On one hand, it can pierce the clouds of depression and doubts away and especially when your motivation pays off and you succeed in what you are trying to achieve.

But what if you do not get what you want? Motivation can end up hurting you by setting yourself up for a fall. This *will* happen if you have also not prepared yourself for the worst.

Preparing yourself for the worst just means that you at least have considered the possibility – and taken the necessary steps for dealing with it.

Tip Number 75: Do it – no matter how long it takes.

It is especially important that you do not give up on your goal just because your route to success turned out to be longer and more twisted than expected. That is the card life has dealt you so deal with it and – again – move on.

Tip Number 76: Do not allow any source of frustration, problems, or depression get worse. Eliminate it right away.

If there is anything troubling you and making it difficult for you to stay focused and motivated – get rid of it right away. Nip it in the bud and do not wait for it to turn into a full-fledged disaster.

Tip Number 77: Think of all those who did not reach as far as you did.

If you were to crow out loud about your victories, then this would be boasting. But you are not. You are just quietly reflecting on how far you have gone and what you have achieved that others cannot.

Sometimes, a person tends to keep on comparing himself to those he feels is better than he is that he fails to realize how much he himself has done more than the others.

When you realize that, you will see for yourself that accomplishing more than others does not make you better. You just happened to be luckier, perhaps, or more patient. The same goes for those who have done more than you.

Motivation is also a matter of time. You will get your goal – you just must work hard and keep your eyes on your destination.

Lightning Source UK Ltd.
Milton Keynes UK
UKHW020141281220
375839UK00009B/341